NATURE'S GIANTS

BISON

BY MARISSA KIRKMAN

WWW.APEXEDITIONS.COM

Apex is distributed by North Star Editions:
sales@northstareditions.com | 888-417-0195

Produced for Apex by Red Line Editorial.

Photographs ©: Shutterstock Images, cover, 1, 4–5, 6, 7, 8–9, 10–11, 13, 14–15, 16–17, 19, 20–21, 22–23, 24, 25, 29; Wildlife GmbH/Alamy, 12; Photo-Fox/Alamy, 18; iStockphoto, 26–27

Library of Congress Control Number: 2023921543

ISBN
978-1-63738-932-4 (hardcover)
978-1-63738-972-0 (paperback)
979-8-89250-066-1 (ebook pdf)
979-8-89250-030-2 (hosted ebook)

Printed in the United States of America
Mankato, MN
082024

NOTE TO PARENTS AND EDUCATORS

Apex books are designed to build literacy skills in striving readers. Exciting, high-interest content attracts and holds readers' attention. The text is carefully leveled to allow students to achieve success quickly. Additional features, such as bolded glossary words for difficult terms, help build comprehension.

CHAPTER 1

GRAZING GIANTS 4

CHAPTER 2

MASSIVE MAMMALS 10

CHAPTER 3

HABITAT 16

CHAPTER 4

BIG BABIES 22

COMPREHENSION QUESTIONS • 28

GLOSSARY • 30

TO LEARN MORE • 31

ABOUT THE AUTHOR • 31

INDEX • 32

CHAPTER 1

GRAZING GIANTS

A huge bison grazes in a field. It chews on grass and weeds as it walks. Insects fly around the bison. They bite its skin.

Bison spend 9 to 11 hours eating each day.

The bison uses a hoof to kick the ground. Then it rolls around in the dirt. This is called wallowing. It stops insects from biting.

Wallowing creates a layer of dirt around a bison's body. The dirt blocks insects.

A bison's long winter fur starts falling out in patches in the spring.

WINTER COATS

Thick fur keeps bison warm during winter. In the spring, bison shed their heavy coats. Rolling on the ground can help remove the fur.

Wallowing also creates a dip in the ground. The bison lies down in the cool soil. After a short rest, it goes back to grazing.

Sometimes, male bison wallow to show off their strength.

CHAPTER 2

MASSIVE MAMMALS

Bison are large **mammals**. Full-grown males may weigh more than 2,000 pounds (900 kg). They stand more than 6 feet (1.8 m) tall.

Female bison are slightly smaller than males.

Bison have huge heads and long, shaggy coats. Their fur is very thick around their heads and front legs. They also have short horns.

Male bison sometimes use their horns to fight.

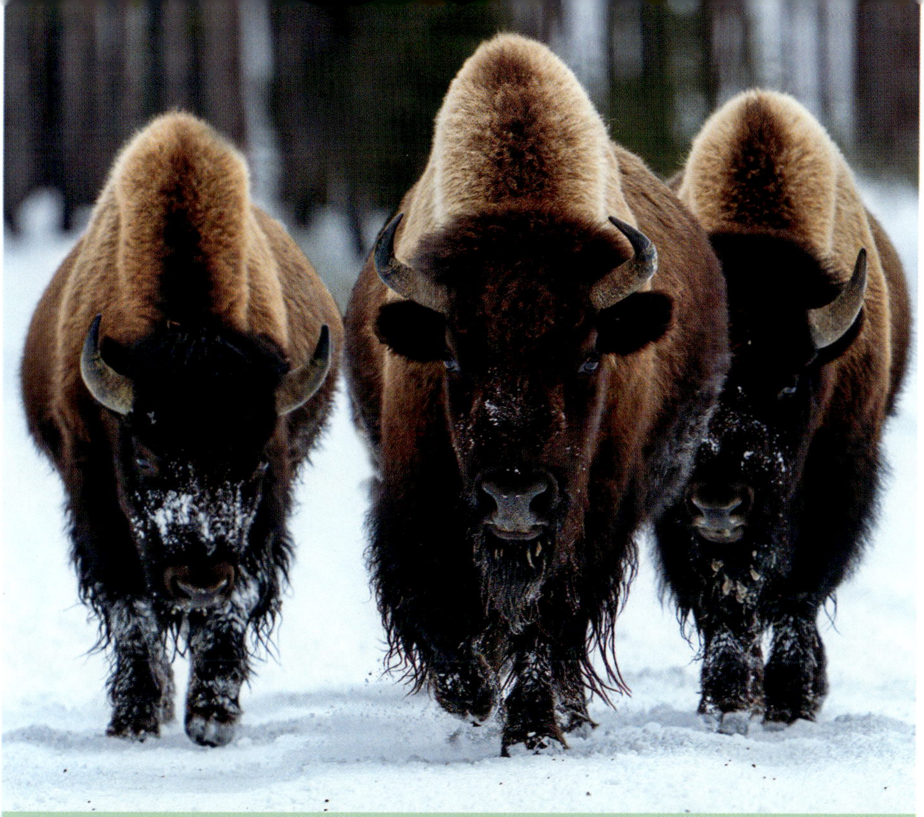

Bison have large humps on their shoulders. The humps are made of muscles.

FAST FACT

During winter, bison swing their heads in the snow to find food. Their horns plow through the snow.

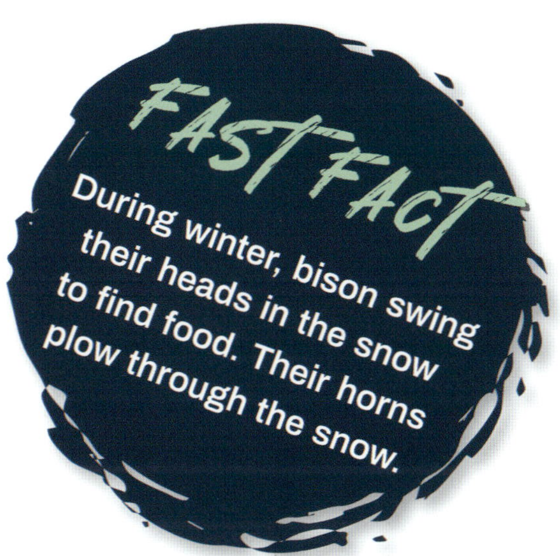

Bison are **herbivores**. They mostly eat grasses and weeds. They also eat leaves and twigs.

Bison eat in the same field for a few days. Then they move to find a new one.

CHEWING CUD

Bison spend a lot of time chewing cud. Cud is partly broken-down food from a bison's stomach. Bison spit this food back up. They chew and swallow it again. This process helps them get more **nutrients**.

CHAPTER 3

Bison are found in North America and Europe. In North America, they live on grasslands and **plains**. In Europe, they live in forests.

Bison are the heaviest mammals in North America and Europe.

In the past, bison roamed from Alaska to Mexico. Now, wild bison live only in **protected** areas. These include parks and wildlife **preserves**.

People killed huge numbers of bison during the 1800s.

In 2022, about 30,000 wild bison lived in North America.

ALMOST GONE

Millions of bison used to live in North America. But in the 1800s, many **settlers** built farms and hunted bison. By 1889, bison were almost **extinct**. North America had fewer than 1,000 left at that time.

Bison can run up to 40 miles per hour (65 km/h).

Bison make short migrations each year. They may move up to 70 miles (113 km). They go south during winter. When it warms up in spring, they return to the north.

FAST FACT

Bison usually move slowly. But they may run if they are scared. A stampede is when many bison run together.

CHAPTER 4

BIG BABIES

Bison live in groups called herds. For most of the year, females live together with calves and young males. Adult males live in their own small herds.

Male bison are called bulls.

Most bison calves are born in the spring.

Males look for **mates** each year. Females give birth to one calf at a time. The calves weigh up to 66 pounds (30 kg).

CHANGING COLORS

A newborn bison's coat is reddish-brown. After a couple months, the calf's coat turns brown. This age is also when a bison's horns begin to grow.

Calves can stand and walk soon after they are born.

Calves drink milk from their mothers. After one week, they begin eating grass, too. Calves stay with their mothers for about a year. By age three, young bison can have babies of their own.

Wolves, bears, and mountain lions may hunt bison.

COMPREHENSION QUESTIONS

Write your answers on a separate piece of paper.

1. Write a few sentences describing the main ideas of Chapter 3.
2. Which fact about bison do you think is most interesting, and why?
3. How much food can a bison eat in one day?
   - A. less than 18 pounds (8 kg)
   - B. more than 20 pounds (9 kg)
   - C. more than 2,000 pounds (900 kg)
4. Which food do bison calves eat first?
   - A. milk
   - B. grass
   - C. leaves

5. What does **grazes** mean in this book?

*A huge bison **grazes** in a field. It chews on grass and weeds as it walks.*

A. runs fast
B. eats plants
C. takes a rest

6. What does **shaggy** mean in this book?

*Bison have huge heads and long, **shaggy** coats. Their fur is very thick around their heads and front legs.*

A. short and thin
B. thick and messy
C. soft and white

Answer key on page 32.

GLOSSARY

extinct

No longer living on Earth.

herbivores

Animals that eat mostly plants.

mammals

Animals that have hair and produce milk for their young.

mates

Animals that come together to have babies.

nutrients

Substances that help something grow and be healthy.

plains

Flat areas of land that do not have many trees.

preserves

Areas of land set aside for plants and animals to live and stay safe.

protected

Watched over or kept safe.

settlers

People who move to a new place.

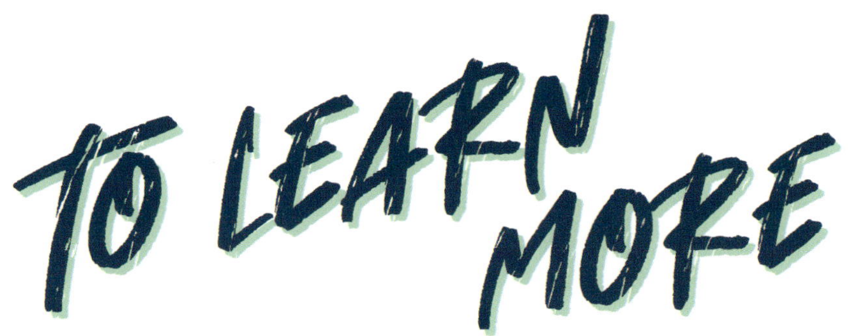

TO LEARN MORE

BOOKS

Duling, Kaitlyn. *Bison*. Minneapolis: Bellwether Media, 2020.

Kenney, Karen Latchana. *Prairies*. Minneapolis: Bellwether Media, 2022.

Kirkman, Marissa. *Biggest Bodies*. Mendota Heights, MN: Apex Editions, 2024.

ONLINE RESOURCES

Visit **www.apexeditions.com** to find links and resources related to this title.

ABOUT THE AUTHOR

Marissa Kirkman is a writer and editor who lives in Illinois. She enjoys reading about animals, science, and history. She once saw wild bison while on a trip to Custer State Park in South Dakota.

INDEX

A
Alaska, 18

C
calves, 22, 24–26
cud, 15

E
Europe, 16
extinct, 19

F
fur, 7, 12

H
herbivores, 14
herds, 22
hoof, 6
horns, 12–13, 25

M
mammals, 10
mates, 24
Mexico, 18
migrations, 21

N
North America, 16, 19

P
preserves, 18

S
settlers, 19
stampede, 21

ANSWER KEY:
1. Answers will vary; 2. Answers will vary; 3. B; 4. A; 5. B; 6. B